THE GO SITUATION

By the same author

True Life Love Stories, Blackstaff Press, 1976
The Irish Frog (imitations from French poetry),
    Ulsterman publications, 1978
The Life of Jamesie Coyle, serialised in *Fortnight* magazine

THE GO SITUATION

MICHAEL FOLEY

BLACKSTAFF PRESS

British Library Cataloguing in Publication Data

Foley, Michael, 1947
  The GO situation.
  I. Title
  821'.914   PR6056.042

ISBN   0–85640–263–X

Published by Blackstaff Press Limited
3 Galway Park, Dundonald, BT16 0AN
with the assistance of
the Arts Council of Northern Ireland

Printed in Northern Ireland by Excel Printing Services

For Martina

Contents

Howdy   1
A provincial adolescence   2
Why I love reason and culture so much   3
Why not come along and give us your views?   4
Young poet   5
The mad scientist   7
The nooks-and-crannies song   9
Solitude   10
Ragtime in the soul   11
Song of the creep   12
The GO situation   14
We must go lightly   15
Brothers and sisters   16
Decision Theory   18
The middle manager in Paradise   20
The world is seldom with us   22
Importunate life   23
Beautiful lofty things   24
Watching striptease and topless go-go in
  the Oxford Tavern, Kentish Town   25
Defilement   26
Yo ho ho!   27
My muse   28
The wife's complaint   29
A dream of unfair women   30
All we dare have   32
The king of Thule   33
Ten years on   35
The in-between song   37
The marriage assizes   39
The coward   40
Negative feedback   41
The power of words to express feelings   43
Corbière's eternal feminine   44

Personal 45
Trees in the wind 47
The linear script 48
On the waterfront 50
The King is half-dead, long live the King! 51
No return 52

Acknowledgements 54

Howdy

Howdy doody, folks. No disrespect
but we'll have to start with some straight talk.
How can you say these things of me?
Me the bitter and cynical sort?
My loving mockery doesn't hurt.
It's a kind of caress for Chrissake.
That's how they court where I come from
– the girl you throw snowballs at
is the one who turns you on.
As for 'anger' – I'm not even slightly upset.
I don't get my crap in an uproar
don't go hairy-assed apeshit
('aplomb in the midst of irrational things').
Whatever you do it's alright with me.
Love you all madly, you dumb assholes!

A provincial adolescence

His nights in the aunts' house, their talk and tea:
who can trace a line back like they can?
They cover the district faster than Tarzan
family tree to family tree

and keep track of their own who're away
– Father Tim's tapes from the Far East:
It's O'Doherty's mince I miss most.
Laughter. Shrieks. It's as good as a play.

They prefer it like this, indoors, the fire on
with their 3-tiered cake-stands for 3-course snacks
legs apart, enjoying the crack
(he fancies the youngest one).

'Don't be getting an eye for the girls whatever you do.
Get all your degrees
and they'll be running after *you.*'
They give him a briefcase for getting an A and two Bs.

Are there men by any chance?
The men doze in chairs
while the women sort out their affairs
– an extreme case of aunts-in-the-pants.

And in summer the big two-car day trips
aunts crammed in the back, at the wheel glum men.
The men have no say in destination or stops.
They have to bolt their ice cream and drive on again.

Why I love reason and culture so much

It's because they were such a part of my heritage.
I was steeped in both from an early stage.

Reason ruled at the R.D.G. (Religious
Discussion Group). The issues were serious:

The morality of the Twist, keeping company after dark.
Discussing winklepickers Sean McGillan made his mark:

'It's not that I'm wildly conservative
But I don't hold with shoes you can pick a lock with'.

Culture was Siobhan McKenna's one-woman show:
Stephens, O'Casey, Synge – stuff to set Irish hearts aglow.

Father Hegarty up on stage, proud but sincere:
'A cultural Siberia they call us here . . .'

Long pause, his fine head high in the light
'. . . *We've proved them wrong tonight'.*

Why not come along and give us your views?

'But you're so destructive'
Fuzzy Bear said
'*con*- and not *dee*-structive
is what you should be

so why not come along
and give us your views?'
He was trying to get me
to speak in the school debates:

That This House believes that
the Law is an Ass or *That Marks*
and Spencer have done more for Man
than Marx and Engels ever did.

Young poet

My biro – *quick*! I thought I saw
in the flowing robes of hairspray ads
Fame with her strange eyes beckoning.
She's a lady can't wait.

Today sees an actor's
biography launched and there's
Wet Fartz recording their
album in Studio Five.

What if I used a little craft
to write the stuff that's read?
Of course I'd have to go austere
belying my twenty years

to work the aged-master style
renting a holiday cottage and writing
of animals, peasants and flowers
with 'fastidious craftsmanship'

getting 'texture' enough to be
used on exams, the bits in
italics referred to in serious
O level questions below:

Indicate what the poet means . . .
What impression is conveyed . . .
An impression of
painstaking boredom, I'm afraid.

Not for me pit ponies
badgers, old snaps or
the albeit heart-rending
scream of a slaughtered pig.

Nor do I see myself
honoured in recognition
of my 'lasting contribution
to aunts-and-uncles poetry'.

Let the massed ranks
of young hopefuls try that.
Send in the clones!
(Don't bother – they're here.)

The mad scientist

A scientist for three years without a white coat
Impervious to Christian name and anecdote

Stonewalling everything to nurse my churl grudge.
My laboratory samples turned out black sludge

No doubt from sheer hate. (See what lack of love can do!)
But it didn't take a fizz out of me. A few

Grains here, a few there. Yes, I cheated. I STOLE!
Ken Cheeseman had heaps – and Dickie Pink (asshole)

But you couldn't cheat at the board. A big lady-
Doctor type shot the questions in and made me

Look like shit. *Cephalins? Uh. Furanose ring? Uh.
Monuron?* Uh. CAN YOU TELL US ANYTHING? Uh.

I was hauled up. He ignored me to jot in neat
Small script, with a good pen, a few lines on each sheet.

His hands and nails were very clean. He said: *I'm afraid*
(Eyes flicked away) *you're not going to make the grade.*

Jerking and mumbling, bumping the chairs, I withdrew.
Vile the white corridors I Quasimodoed through.

Things looked bad – but there were lab books still. At this time
Mistakes were in. *Even geniuses in their prime*

*Make mistakes. However unlike us they don't try
To cover up. They love their schemes to go awry.*

*It makes them think. It's how they learn. That small mistake
That you and I would ignore can bring the big break.*

Thus experiments had to be worked out – in the light
Of investigated mistakes. Right, I said. *Right.*

A new lab book under my arm I took the long way
Home through an empty park. *Human mistakes.* OK.

This is what they want. *Authentic errors.* Right.
I waited in my attic room and late at night

It came to me – this . . . *inner truth* – like when you know
It's a great dart even before you make the throw.

I flew Cheeseman and Dickie Pink, the world of men
As plausible human errors flowed from my pen

All so poignant, so touching, so *true.* I almost wept
Myself at them and while the trusting burghers slept

In their chalet-bungalow estates real genius
Flowered in an attic room. It had to be A-plus!

Never had talent like this been used on a mere hoax.
I even wrote in yukky scientific jokes.

That it burned with a true flame would never be known.
Dawn slowly broke. I was . . . alone . . . alone . . . ALONE!

The nooks-and-crannies song

I sing the nooks and crannies of the day.
I sing the intelligent underhand way.
    Summer and Christmas
    Don't hold all the bliss
You can have it all the time with the right ploy
Riding the rush-hour crowd in private joy

Brilliantly silent among the dull chat
Though making sure nobody knows what you're at
    Your face completely composed
    As you yawn with your mouth closed
Or employ that incredible cunning required
To answer correctly a question you haven't heard.

Dissembling too! Grave, with a swirling coffee cup:
How much for a '67 Volks with ten thou up?
    Exuding phoney sense
    As you listen, intense
Observing your toe complete a thoughtful ring
And murmuring *This is it* or *This is the thing.*

How they love the non-existent interplay
Scoffing every fish-head I toss their way
    Though, gauging their dullness
    I toss less and less
Grinning but mentally slipping away.
I sing the nooks and crannies of the day!

Solitude

How I loved solitude! I'd emerge from
a three-day stretch half crazed. (*Cauld balls*
I was called.) Such indulgence is bad.
You get sweaty, unshaven, unreal, sick of books.
Even Greats disagree and none has what you want
scouring shelves for the one you ought to write.
It's like boozing or love or competitive games
– best the sweet time snatched against the odds.

Stick in a job and you may get a lair.
Ah the hours in my lair! Though God knows it's
not much – without water and see-through in front
so the boss can come on me (and often has)
my feet spread, with a mystical gaga look
like a businessman whipped by a whore.

Ragtime in the soul

'You've got to keep a little ragtime in your soul'
Duke Ellington

Unlike the young frogs I adore
who *épater*-ed the bourgeoisie
and died, I am digging
in for a long stretch.

I don't want to go out
in a blaze of scorn
or dribble away
in tubercular angst.

I want to see how it works out
the novelist's sense of time
as well as the lyric poet's Now
(they all say I should stick to prose).

Protective coloration's
what the young frogs lacked
– I blend with my peer group
like pest on a leaf.

I've even launched a b.f.u.
(*bourgeois family unit* to you)
which I support from *halfway up Scale Three*.
(Deceive and eat, the poet says.)

I think I know how to
preside with a poker face
the ragtime held in the soul
as the Duke advised.

Art has its role too
not moaning or gushing
but giving strength – not *dernier*
but forty-denier verse.

Song of the creep

I don't do but I know (Oh-ho!)
I know, I know, I know, I know, I know!
  That's the point of creepy ways
    The hours with books
    The dreamy looks.
Did you think I'd emerge half-blind, half-crazed
  A fool stumbling round in a daze?
    Knowledge makes you *glow*.

All one-girl creeps forego, I know.
We don't get a lot – but we're not so slow.
  We stick with the knack and will.
    Hunt change and range
    With sexy strange
You'll find few can stroke a cock with skill
  So rare and underrated still
    As Gavin Ewart showed.

I don't act but I see (Hee-hee!)
And the opting-out's not for young eyes, believe me.
  Even artists don't need to be coaxed.
    Poetic slobs
    Grab culture jobs
And kill time with coffee and practical jokes
  Wits deployed on the latest hoax
    ('That phone call was *me*.')

Who'd guess my home-town's mess?
It's not big-bellied villains exploiting distress
  But my peers, once students all scorn
    And the duller lot,
    The drones – guess what?
Now teach where they were thumped and spurned
  Going hairy-assed apeshit in turn
    – Though I couldn't care less.

I see and laugh (Not half!)
Avoiding any *saeva indignatio* stuff.
  Who'd heed me? Anyway it palls.
    No satirist
    I insist
Just to see and assimilate it all
  Crowds out spite and gall.
    Too much is enough.

The GO situation

We ought to be philosophers
reducing in a crucible
but also avid gossipers
delighting in the usual.

You can't cut discussion
with sobering clinchers
or guard a position
with Doberman pinschers.

You can't lock your soul
in a gold tabernacle
avoiding your role
in the sordid debacle.

You can't make a Hamlet
without breaking eggs
and must run the gauntlet
on tired aching legs

which doesn't really hurt you
however many say so
– nor do you need grim virtue
enduring with a halo.

Going blithely's far more fruitful
exploring deeper strata
getting your ass out of nootral
and analysing the data.

No, your life's not wasted running
errands like a blue-assed fly
lost in sordid slumming
while the finer things pass by.

You're not below your station
debased and ripped off
– it's a GO situation
and you have lift-off.

We must go lightly

Christ, what a shock! (I was white as a priest's ass.)
To be knocked clean across the class
By a shoulder charge from a girl!
Micky, how do ye stand this mess?
– Joe Mackie, now selling insurance for Pearl.

I have borne things that shattered other men's dreams.
Triumphant, I wade the remedial streams
(The ore's underneath all right
Though in some very awkwardly situated seams).
In the end you can always sleep at night.

Checking a rampant class
Is tougher than holding a mountain pass
But – you see?– I returned from the dead
To come on strong and kick ass.
We must go lightly, without dread.

Brothers and sisters

No, not writers for Heaven's sake. That bunch of slobbers
    Are nobody's brothers.
      It's a secret, I shouldn't say
      But they're mostly *t..h..i..c..k.*
They've read little, know less. Sick, sour and full of booze
    They're locked out of Heaven
      And nothing consoles them, not even
    The big print their prestigious publishers use.

My brothers rarely write though they've intelligence and fun.
    Most jobs have one
      Tucked away, detached and wry
      Knowing just when to catch your eye
During a.o.b. at the A.G.M. as they move to split the motion
    Into five separate parts
      Before debating and voting starts
    A motion on methods of coffee-money collection.

Or at those lovely moments when people give the game away
    Some status-seeker, say
      Affecting to scorn petty worry
      For love of jokes, Indian curry
Parties, booze and sex — *until someone else gets promotion*
    When you glimpse the real man
      Beneath the Monty Python fan
    Such flashes of revelation the headiest potion.

How they love wisdom, my brothers, open to any question
    Yet full of discretion
      Never trying to make you booze
      Pressure and lack of time excused
(We'll be free in a better age, as Cavafy used to say).
    Like icebergs, with $7/8$ below
      But not cold as icebergs. No, no
Warm, the warmth coming through in its indirect way.

And sisters? Those as well, discussing the usual bothers
    Husbands and lovers
   Who go or won't go, stay or won't stay
   Awkward and hurtful either way.
Women always tell you more, not obsessed with hiding pain.
    Instead of the usual bland crap
    Genuine goodies fall in your lap
  Bizarre, funny and intimate knowledge of men.

The warmth was direct then. It would make a sated prince moan
    The sweet nights I've known.
   They've jostled the post-sherry queue
   To get next to me at the staff do
Flesh fragrant with good scent, carefully made-up and dressed
    Not just agreeing with, *fancying* too
    Turning my insides to warm goo
  Eyes locked on mine, holding them, really impressed.

Decision Theory

I was skulking in my eyrie
Letting things go from bad to worse
Projecting zero growth, risk averse
Until I discovered Decision Theory.

Now watch me check out a hunch
Traversing a decision tree
With simian agility
Selecting the optimal branch

Then preparing the right sales pitch
And going into the market place
With a bright enthusiastic face
To sell to some son of a bitch.

Of course we'll never *be* the same
But what could be more stylish
Than joining in with fantastic relish
Beating the world at its own game

Spreading dismay and confusion
By having an indecent hard-on
For management-science jargon?
A new satire – *manic collusion*!

Excelling at hard-necked barter
And faking the sheen of success
No dosser who couldn't care less
A 'results-oriented self-starter'.

How I flummoxed the interview board!
My Expected Monetary Value
Was pretty hot, I can tell you
After some of the points I scored.

Unnerve them with 'inner resources'
Bursting with piss and vinegar
An affront to every manager
On the in-service courses

Coming tops on the simulation
Amazing the timid and gauche
With your Interactive Approach
To Multi-Criterion Optimisation!

The middle manager in Paradise

Homeostasis finally. System oscillation over. All parameters at rest.
I have my eternal reward for doing my best

Well earned, with squeezes and cuts and harmonious working
  relations to foster
In a time of eroded differentials and deficit-staffing posture

With regular breakdown of normative order, colleagues who
  couldn't care less
A total absence of structured complementarity in the interaction
  process.

Here it is at last – peace and space with nothing to spoil it
Like running out of tins or having to empty a chemical toilet

And if solitude and empty places give me the blues
There's the first nights, launchings, openings and anniversary do's.

No need to panic, heaping your plate at the smorgasbord
You can go back as many times as you like and nobody says a word

Unlimited red/white, sweet/dry sploshing out of your glass in the
  fray
Crushed up against beautiful women who, far from turning away

Agree to oral sex when accosted, taking on all comers
And serving them any number of times (single swallows don't make
  summers).

Every taste is catered for. There's cutprice SM centres stocking every
  line
Braziers, branding-irons, manacles, self-assembly torture racks in
  natural pine.

Though no one's exploited really and of course there's no brutality.
Everyone has meaningful relationships and is comfortable in their
  sexuality.

We have consciousness-raising sessions and state-of-the-art
  seminars
Regular small encounter groups to find and remove whatever jars

Recurrent education preventing crises from catching us napping
Creating autonomous learners geared to continuous environment-
  shaping.

No one's exempt from our in-service training. Every six weeks
You attend a hands-on workshop in trouble-shooting techniques

Simulated stress situations assessed by Barry, the young whizz kid:
'I think you were a *shade too directive* there, Ken . . . *unless of course
it was a leadership bid.*'

Barry will keep us results-oriented. Barry won't let us get lax
And take refuge in cognitive dissonance (refusing to face facts)

And anyway God's always popping in to see if everything's all right
Distinguished and reassuring, goateed, with the voice of an acting
  knight

Showing interest, concern and civility (so much rarer and harder
  than love)
And signing his humorous bestselling autobiography *Heavens
Above!.*

The world is seldom with us

The world is seldom with us, late or soon.
We have given our hearts for taste, a sordid boon.
Wimpy Bars and quiz shows, D.I.Y. and pop
    Sing-songs and ices
    And family crises
    Wrinkle our noses
    In yukky poses
Childhood and nature O.K., the rest crap.

I mean, what is this golden-childhood jive?
Life doesn't start till you're twenty-five
The world unfolding year by year.
    Nature's alright (*yawn*)
    But too much is a con.
    Getting natural highs
    From landscapes and skies
Is often a cop-out from life. Not my fear.

Only managers of football teams
Have my range of emotions and dreams:
We are 'choked' or 'sick' or 'over the moon'!
    Though my blurb looks dull
    I have lived to the full:
    Lovers, writers, children, work
    My friends more work than work!
Oh I shouldn't be carping – they're also fun.

How can we ever be stale, in a rut
(Any more than 'blocked' or 'written out')?
How can committed lovers get bored?
    You're a bed crisply made
    A shave with a new blade
    A bag of fresh baps
    A letter with snaps
(Colour ones) big and full on the hall floor!

Importunate life

I haunted the empty parts, the grand front room
Like a Czar's summer palace ablaze with light
(the only vulgar touch the plastic candle grease
on the imitation Louis Quatorze chandeliers)
and the stuffed attic promising secrets, delivering
junk – old photographs, medals, jewellery, lace
though I came on a full box of Dr White's once
– the evidence can't be entirely suppressed.

And importunate life came to bang on the door
– turf, sticks, Betterware, milk, bread, brock.
Brock was waste food for pigs which the brock
men scooped from your bin with the heel
of a stale loaf. They were said to make
sandwiches out of it, perched on their cart.

Beautiful lofty things

The celebration drink for
Una, Eileen, May and Joan
down to their target weights
after weeks of Unislim.

From her bathing-suit's
tight gusset-edge
individual, irrepressible
springy hairs.

Returning from seeing
the babysitter home
– the old street transmuted
important and rare.

Talk waning, the shy wife
bearing it in – warm, golden
highpiled, moist – a loaded plate
of freshly-toasted sliced pan.

Watching striptease and topless go-go in the Oxford Tavern, Kentish Town

It is always sex *or* violence never *and*.
This Oxford Tavern crowd would eat from your hand

Like a hallful of civil servants on a course!
Jackie begins and we feel the terrible force

Of a good high kick. It demolishes the loins
Sucks the soul right out, melts the marrow of the bones!

Elaine, though small and slight, scorns boots for slavegirl thongs
And this is brave – though she's too cerebral and longs

To go off on a ballet-type 'creative' fit.
As the Duke said of (white) Juan Tizol: *too legit*.

At ten o'clock the first strip – as usual, artless
And overdone, coarse burlesque turns with no finesse.

In place of the needling piquancies of the dance
Liz steals our spectacles and shoves them down her pants.

Though it has its worth, spurring Jackie on to climb
New dizzy heights – Jackie James in her fearful prime

Playfully toying with us in the mocking tone
Of a Tricky Sam Nanton solo on trombone

Then exploding madly across the stage again
In wild and fervent arabesques that leave us drained.

Even the hitman type in jungle hat and shades
Is reduced to mush by the time the music fades

For contrary to what we're led to understand
It is always sex *or* violence never *and*.

Defilement

after Rimbaud

Brutes once fucked on the run from behind
Arhythmically slamming it in to the bag
Teaching our forefathers how to shag
Trailing ribbons of juice in the raw wind

And even if some codpieces weren't full
(They had no Trade Descriptions Act)
The middle ages didn't lack
The means or the will.

Today's family man lies
In a stupor of fantasies
Stirring at length

To zip open his flies
Experienced protection-wise
Nappy liners best for wet strength.

Yo ho ho!

With few writers to discover
    And our paltry souls laid bare
Male talk stirs no zest or wonder
    Only women make me care.
Fifteen men for a live girl's chest
Yo ho ho and a gallon of come!

Crude male sex-drive peaks in mid-teens
    Woman's builds to twenty-eight
Ours in roughness, heavings, gropings
    Theirs in richness flowering late.
Fifteen men for a low-necked dress
Yo ho ho and a gallon of come!

Wives and mothers, toil and worry
    Checks and loss enrich their love.
Let me say it straight out – it's my
    Sisters-in-law I'm full of.
Fifteen men for a lewd caress
Yo ho ho and a gallon of come!

Looks! Looks! In their eyes' ignored depths
    All the power of the baulked – fire
Stamina, tenderness, skill (perhaps
    Even *les choses bizarres*).
Fifteen men for a hot groin-press
Yo ho ho and a gallon of come!

Back off! DANGER! Complexities!
    We know what we can't do
(Mature attractiveness is wise).
    Looks I love though . . . coarse words too.
Fifteen men for some near-incest
Yo ho ho and a gallon of come!

My muse

No, you couldn't be more wrong. She's not a looker
Or a nympho, tossing it up like a hooker

Not wildly young with scarcely a hair on her bump
Or luridly old, a notorious arty hump

Not a paid-up and card-carrying patron of art
Or some 'pure' outsider like an e.s.n. tart.

She's just an average woman who's been in the wars
With a spare tyre, stretch marks and operation scars

Experienced and wary, not expecting much
Disillusioned concerning men – though not gone butch

Still cherishing a dream of how it ought to be:
Some day my prince will come at the same time as me.

I could show her, performing with selfless care
All delicate sensitive foreplay, timing and flair

Tenderly tasting and savouring down to the dregs
Wiping the memory of brutes who jumped on like clegs.

Whoa, there! The commitments, the needs and demands.
Between hers and mine both we'd do well to hold hands

For ten minutes in some scruffy park. Yes, it's tough.
But the presence of goodness is often enough.

Just to feel it, however briefly, in the air
And to know afterwards it's around somewhere.

Not to get proving your own worth isn't the worst.
Protected souls atrophy. You have to live first.

If we don't go the whole way (a most likely if)
I'm still grateful for getting deliciously stiff.

The wife's complaint

I went of my own will a bride to the south.
None but myself chose this life here
where our new row dwindles to shops and fields
and the grey sky folds its languor
about the spirit with no hope.

Such a 'good home' was lord-love to me.

My sister's lord took her across the sea.
Wary of life-match, refusing to plan
they said he would never settle down.
I too thought he was no good:
He'll walk the feet off that wee girl.

Now they go free while I breed and rear
– two in the house and my lord wanting more.

There's my little pair, running with cries
making friends where they will.
If only it didn't drag the parents in!

Hateful our neighbours in this grim place.
We worked with some of them freeing a drain
– it was our condoms blocking it up!
Hundreds of them, swollen, floating there.
We didn't know where to look.

Perhaps things will turn out all right
– like my second, sitting wrong way up
but appearing head first in the end.

My sister's young lord says it's so.
Brilliant his eyes on my eyes when we meet.
Bell-clear and strong his laughter and mocking sport.

It would be good to have that young lord once
naked and smiling beside my bed
his slender fragrant body near my head
– I under the covers already
so the stretch marks wouldn't show!

29

A dream of unfair women

I was shagged from slaving at work all day.
The plan was to tackle a bit of Proust
Or *The New York Review Of Books* at least
But I lay on the sofa and dozed off . . .

Whereupon this angry woman appeared
A hulking diesel dyke with such a look
I thought she was going to punish me.
Just an order (alas!): *Get off your butt.*
I was whipped away to the local hall
Just after a Boys' Club and Bingo night
Spittle and fag-ends tramped into the floor
And tobacco smoke hanging in dim light
– But the passion there put drabness to flight.
It was poets' wives spoiling for a fight!
Just one wretched poet shaking with fright
His wife relentlessly hammering in:
'So this is the life you lead writing verse
Solemn poems in the aged-master style
Then flattery, boozing and dirty jokes
In the scramble for cushy jobs and perks.
Lovers of art? You don't even read books
Or only each others' to keep in touch.
It's always in public the reading is
Your own stuff, boomed out, fifty quid a time
Invited to Guinness parties after
The show (Guinness family, not the drink)
Easy cash and fame – and a bit of strange
Some girl you can write a poem-sequence on
– Wild falling in and anguished wriggling out
The bits everyone wants to hear about.
So honest and moving! How you poets feel!'
And what does he manage in self-defence?
'It's the price of my gift.' That got a laugh.
Then they went to work – not a pretty sight –
And when they were done with him turned on me.

'Now hold on,' I said 'what you say's all right
But fair's fair – yrs. tly. isn't like that.
I don't give readings – or even go out
And who's worked as hard in a steady job
Positions of trust, the respect of peers?
Me running round after a bit of strange?
I've lumbered two women in thirty years.'
They were not impressed. 'Hear his righteousness.
Off to the writing room every night
The sex on the page and the wife left bored.
Did I say writing room? Hah! *Wanking* room.
Hunched over his table, tearing away
Coffee cooling and MSS ignored.
Known as a cocksman (and even feared!) – but
Always engrossed in wee poems or too tired,
Even cutting his measly weekend treat
If he has a few beers or stays up late.'
This was the signal: 'Cauld balls!' 'Turd!' 'Is a
Scared mammy's boy going to shock us with
Dirty words?' 'We'll see who's shocked when we start.'
They were right – it was running down my legs
Wet noodles unable to take a step.
I wanted to scream – but no sound got out.
A Mothercare catalogue split my mouth!

Then I woke in my flat. No wife! No child!
She's left me I thought – but it all came back.
It was keep-fit night. Jane was fast asleep.
Look at the time though! So much to be done
A clean shirt to find and a lunch to make.

All we dare have

It's a notion commonly
held by seekers after truth
that restlessness is energy
and turbulence means worth

but I hate an 'artistic' fuss
where women, pets and children
(the legitimate ones that is)
vie with disciples dropping in.

Life is small or I am small
(and this is a prospect
facing us all)
but what I detect

in the gay ballyhoo
is the mute pain of the wife.
There is no way you
can be larger than life.

All we dare have of the dream
is to mix with ordinary folk
but not being quite what we seem
cause a little conjectural talk.

The king of Thule

after Laforgue

There was an ironic king of Thule
    An ironic king was he.
He laughed at his staff's corrupt misrule
At his ministers playing him for a fool
    (He called them his fiddlers three)

But his jibes at his faithless queen were worse
    – Well known as hot stuff
Her appetities insatiable and coarse
(Like Catherine the Great shagged to death by a horse).
    The king laughed his peg off.

Of course no one else saw the joke.
    It was much too *noir*.
After all his subjects were ordinary folk
Who thought there'd be tears when a heart broke.
    At last it went too far.

The king climbed alone to his ivory tower
    Dragging the heavy keys
(It was locked and burglar-alarmed). For hours
He worked on a silk sail covered with flowers.
    Only the stars could see

When he finished his last embroideries
    And raising his sail
Rowed hard across the grey seas
Towards the sun in its final agonies
    Emitting this strange wail:

    'Dying sun, from dawn to dusk
    Your rays from above
    Draw forth the viviparous lust
    Of the cult which men call love.

'And now before the wild night's flood
As you feel your senses fail
With a last drop of martyr's blood
You are cleaning the altar rail.

'Dying sun, together we're going down
So let us show some pride.
For the terrible polar palaces I'm bound
To wrap your heart in a silk shroud.'

Thus he cried, upright and handsome on deck
    Though dreadfully upset
As towards the reefs and sunken wrecks
Mocked and unmanned by the gentler sex
    A grim course he set.

Lovers, remember him when you'd play it cool
    Secure in irony.
If you can't mix in like the average fool
You might end up like that king of Thule.
    A warped old king was he.

Ten years on

Something formal and grand, elaborate, terribly well done
    Apart from the rest of the oeuvre
Neither lightweight nor flip, the big fat stanzas surging on
    A regular Amazon
    Inexorable though not seeming to move
– The appropriate scale for a wedding gift ten years late
Though it must have feeling too, enough to compensate

For all the crazy rules I made – what was not to be done
    Decreed in a headmaster's way:
The mandatory evening silence, the banning of Radio One
    The cutting all fun
    From our wretched wedding day
– Even then too mean-spirited, priggish and cold:
Invite one of those cunts and it's off you were told.

I'd have them all there now – now I've changed my ways –
    The difficult, boring and dopey
Fed alike, then speeches of corny jokes and fulsome praise
    And revels lasting two days
    Gropes and fights and the hokey-pokey
Danced to a loud hick band, my left leg out, my left leg in
Finally collapsing over a table of half-finished gin.

Yes I've slowed down, come to terms – which might be news
    To some. *Give it time* was the cry
Meaning gaps would show up, arty groupies come to confuse.
    Oh those ego-masseuses
    With their sweet rubdown! Who can deny
Their skill, knowing just what you want? *You're so honest*
Was gushed at me once. Not sex, but flattery's the test.

Only knowledge helps. As you say, I'm a devious swine.
    Knowledge and wisdom we'll get.
You too. 'Not an articulate girl but wise'. If you don't shine
    In public it's fine.

Confusion's becoming in some sets
And I've never prized social success (though you doubt
Me on this). When you walked in the anecdotes ran out.

Come away with me! Alone, we'll sing in our prison too
    Not annoyed, full of mischievous glee
Having all the latest gossip sent – who sneaked a screw
      Who's leaving who
    The rancour, rage and jealousy
Love in all its manifestations, compelling and crude
Screams, tears, fracas, even blows (by me just one, *touch wood*).

The in-between song

It's falling in love people love, the nervous excitement
Move and counter-move in the ancient game of enticement

But I don't yearn for early days with their permanent state
Of tumescence, prepared to get up on a cracked plate

Smoothtalking my way into your house and fumbling on chairs
Jumping away in fright at a bronchial cough upstairs

Returning through dark deserted streets, pounding on like crack
Troops on the march – or hobbling in agony, foreskin back

Getting home again at dawn and trying not to wake a soul
By peeing in total darkness down the side of the bowl.

Nor do I yearn to be free, casting off wasted years
To ride someone else into the sunset with joyful tears.

So that's NO bap-faced students, NO culture vultures in heat
NO colleagues or in-laws seeing my true worth, NO *dark meat*

NO petulant nymphets, detached and impossibly slim
NO mature divorcees with it biting the leg off them

NO receptionists taking off glasses and letting down hair
NO frustrated green-belt wives in expensive underwear

– Strictly for Wednesday Plays. Real ones are tough as old hide.
There's little glamour truly. As my old friend gently sighed

Of Marilyn Monroe: *How could the Kennedy boys get*
Excited? Her poor little thing wouldn't even be wet.

Then there's phoney free-form passion, ripping skin and yelling.
I favour standards, traditional grammar and spelling

Calm organisation and planning, the disciplined way
(See my 'Top-down Methodology in Structured Sex Play').

You're my centre of excellence with private grounds in bloom
Resource and reception areas, hospitality room

My new in-house system with hands-on capability
User-friendly, with feedback, power and flexibility

Affording continuous two-way communication
My optimal target group for market penetration

My core- and flexi-time, my rest and recreation
My ongoing, upwardly mobile situation.

My love will survive all troubles, the fighting and bitching
Huffs, depressions, illnesses and personal-membrane itching

The ravages of time, of course. Decrepit, fat or thin
I will never be unsure which wrinkle to put it in.

Tumultuous, piquant, the start and the end of the thing
Are the bits that sell – but the in-between time's what I sing

The lights low and half the band gone for their tea and a bun.
We take the floor again. The number is a smoochy one.

The marriage assizes

The marriage assizes are held every day
        And every thing you say
Can be taken down and used in evidence
Though the badness is more of tone than sense.
        It's a subtle game
        And no one courts blame.
Only mugs and newly-weds make a straight play.

And don't think a jury of friends, however true
        However close to you
Can be looked to for justice. Friends feel
And are prone to emotional appeal.
        They bog down in the mire
        They get caught in crossfire
No nearer to finding out who's screwing who.

Nor do past cases help, with issues so fudged
        Such refusals to budge
(I don't like conceits but I'm stuck with this now)
And who'd accept the verdict anyhow?
        It would carry no clout.
        'You talked your way out.'
'You fluttered your eyes at the silly old judge.'

The coward

More under control but less
Wise, what I think
Slips through my cageyness
Only when I drink

All the grudges I hoard
In a torrent you can't resist.
The brave man does it with a sword
The coward when he's pissed.

Negative feedback

Black was my darling's mood
Scorning all I ever did.
Indeed it wouldn't look good
On the Blake-Mouton grid:

High points for productiveness
Zero for human relations.
Most of them ended in joyless
Fatigue and frustration.

Emotional coldness – that's my disease
Lukewarm about peer-group bonding
Generating doubt and unease
Instead of freely responding.

And bad investment policy
Leads to market penetration.
These days brand loyalty
Won't stave off competition.

But just hold your horses
Honey! Give me a while
To go on executive courses
And learn participative style.

There'll be changes, you'll see
At the end of each week
An hour of P.E.R.T.
(Program Evaluation & Review Technique).

This won't be a system closed
In a sterile determinism
I'll stroke every motion proposed
To see if we get any jism.

I'll play the democratic role
And consult the grass roots
Running everything up the pole
To see if anyone salutes.

No more playing to win
Dogmatic and sarky
I'll be stepping down in
The dominance hierarchy

Sweet-talking assholes all day
And looking as if I really care
Lovably bright as a DJ
Allowing no dead air.

A rebuilding determined
Progressive and durable
On the scale of the German
Economic miracle!

With a noose round your neck
And your feet on the trap door
Negative feedback
Is something you can't ignore.

The power of words to express feelings

When she left him he couldn't find a single word
    And when she came back one sufficed.
       Christ, it was. *Christ! Oh Christ!*
Blessed is he that comes in the name of the Lord.

Corbière's eternal feminine

On our backs you crack the whip of your caprice
Allowing us pleasures vivid but fleeting
Before the swift permanent fall from grace
To insomnia, booze and compulsive eating

Raiding the late-night delicatessen
For cream cakes and Black Forest gateau
– Though the sorrow and pain don't lessen
As the black night wears on, long and slow.

Bitch curled up foetus-wise
Fitting against your stud with sighs
May you learn what it's like to weep

With clenched teeth in impotent fury
Mouth tasting of horse-blanket puree
Even tossing off bringing no sleep.

Personal

Straight guy (30s) getting head
Together after bad trip
Seeks giving chick (30s, own pad)
With view sex/companionship.

Professional type, understanding
Polite, without sexual kinks
(Strictly no buggery, branding
Or wanting his bag nailed to planks)

Physically in his prime
And well cared-for health-wise
Bran-fed, with a fast transit time
And above-average stool size

Good talker, easy adapter
Well-read and smart (it's no fool
Who can go a whole chapter
With one of the Frankfurt School)

Yet never too highbrow or stuffy
To try something lighter
– Laughing wildly over coffee
Through the Gate's bad-taste all-nighter

Or going to see a live band
And being frenzied or laidback
An appropriately-zonked fan
Of *Scumbag* or *Fuck You Jack*.

An escort up with fashion
Game – you could do a lot worse.
Just don't expect the impassioned
Exuberant youth of his verse

The blithe spreader of praise and blame
Among the little magazines
Sorting everyone out, the champagne
Of insouciance filling his veins.

That bright sureness wears away
Impulses, duties rubbing together
Inexorably, gradually
Taking the shine off each other.

You're reliable and competent
— But the champagne's lost its fizz.
It's not that you can't get what you want
You no longer know what it is.

Trees in the wind

Look at those trees! Hard not to think
they're expressing your feelings
whatever they are. Self-piteous
probably. Those who watch them from
rain-flecked windows aren't action men.
Lust for freedom, guilt . . . such things.
What are they saying to me?
'We are soldiering on here
doing our thing in the growing dark
complex, interrelated, ignored.'

The linear script

The true state of adult affairs
Is the sick soul, confused and loath
'Dull dims of unapparent growth'
Sick children, bills and nostril hair.

To be back when things were simple
And the height of naughtiness was
Some floozie asking Kirk Douglas
How he shaved his dimple!

To start young as Brandon de Wilde in *Shane*
And live life to a linear script
High as a kite on hero worship
When Alan Ladd rides in over the plain

Such a symbol of life and adventure
That poor mom is sopping wet too
– Though of course she can't ride off like you
To become a romantic figure

The solitary prone to attacks
Of black brooding, tough, taciturn
Volatile, deep – Brando's slow burn
And blow-out in *One-Eyed Jacks*

Saying nothing to each nasty dig
Then with a terrifying quiver
Violently throwing the table over:
Get up, you scum-suckin' pig.

Free rein to every emotion
That's the script we all want
Someone else bearing the brunt
With a dog-like devotion

Some Mexican beauty for instance
Untainted by dreams of dissension
Depressions, pre-menstrual tension
Or wilful delayed adolescence

Nothing but virginal purity
Coaxing you on to your goal
That most impossible of all
Uncomplex, folksy maturity

Gently pushing aside the gun
In the hand of the hot-headed kid
Without batting an eyelid
Growling: *That isn't the answer, son.*

On the waterfront

There can be no such thing as a life
that wasn't meant for the person who has it.
Louis Simpson

We think our loved ones pull us under
       So unfairly
Interfering with demands that end our
       High hopes early.
I could have been a contender.
       It was you, Charlie.

We're always handed loaded dice
       In this vale of woe.
It's not your night, kid. We're going for the price.
       How well we know
Charlie's unignorable advice.
       – But is it so?

Could Terry have taken Wilson apart
       As he thought?
Did he really have the heart
       For a title shot
– Or were we biased from the start
       By a strong crude plot?

You should never blame an outcome
       On conditions
Or people. When you end up a bum
       Breeding pigeons
Accept the fault's your own dumb
       Cowardly decisions.

The King is half-dead, long live the King!

Fancy us carrying *him* shoulder-high
Philip Larkin our King of Parnassus
A frightened creep, stingy and dry
Never living and now scared to die
The thought of going up to God without his glasses
Even less fun than despising the masses.

Cold hearts can speak and little men
Can win the bays – bearing witness
Like scary Philip's, harsh and plain
In the way criticism can't explain
That mysterious simplicity and flatness
That carries such intensity and aptness.

No return

My madly misogynist Nietzschean friend
Who hated reason, all things planned
Now writes to complain of his native land:
Their lack of civics drives me round the bend.
Broken homes, Micky my other friend said
When three louts cracked a chair on his head.

Even if we know we're less fun
More inclined to give a lecture
And when contradicted, hector
Even if we'd like out it can't be done.
I want to *scream* – but there's no return
To callow youth. A terrible duty is born.

Acknowledgements

Some of these poems have appeared in *The Honest Ulsterman,*
Fortnight, The London Review of Books, Encounter, The Times
Literary Supplement, The Irish Press, Gown, Stoneferry Review,
Jam, Linewords and *The Niagara Magazine.*